MurMurings
Including "Funny Tales of Terror" and other desperate cries for help

Murray Siegel

This page purposely left blank.
For insurance purposes.
You'll get it later.

If you read the text above,
you shouldn't have.
Because this is a blank page.

MurMurings

Dedicated with love to my wife Karen, my parents, and Ben.

> "As he spoke, the pastry-cook tried to take from the old lady the small box, which she had put in one of her pockets."
>
> Honore De Balzac
>
> "Murray, is that story ready for Ted yet???"
>
> Mary Richards
>
> "It's pronounced Ball Zack. Zack. ZACK. Got it? What's wrong with you people? I'm never doing THIS again!"
>
> Honore De Balzac
>
> "I'm so glad I have a fairly normal last name."
>
> Charles Dickens

MurMurings

Other books by Murray Siegel

Front Cover Photo: Kristopher Roller on Unsplash

Copyright © 2021 by Murray Siegel
All rights reserved. No part of this book may be reproduced, scanned
or distributed in any printed or electronic form without permission.
First Edition: September 2021
Printed in the United States of America

MurMurings

Contents

Short stupid stuff	1
Funny Tales of Terror: The Time I Almost Got Robbed	7
More of the short stupid stuff	10
Funny Tales of Terror: When A Dog Bit Me During the 1968 Riots	15
Even more of the short stupid stuff	19
Funny Tales of Terror: The First Time I Had Sex	23
You thought there was no more short stupid stuff?	24
Funny Tales of Terror: The Time I Really Got Robbed	27
There's always more short stupid stuff	33
Funny Tales of Terror: My First Car Accident	35
The short stupid stuff just keeps piling up	37
Funny Tales of Terror: The Time I Nearly Got Struck By Lightning	41
The short stupid stuff takes a turn toward intelligent	44
Funny Tales of Terror: My Kingdom for a Rest Stop	49
The short stupid stuff turns away from intelligent	53
Funny Tales of Terror: Bomb Scary	57
You've completed the short stupid stuff	61
Funny Tales of Terror: The Time I Got Crushed By A Giant	63

MurMurings

Introduction

"MurMurings" is mostly a compilation of my Facebook posts that first started in 1991, many years before the invention of Facebook. You may notice that they are clean and meant to be enjoyed by family members of all ages. In fact, not once is the word "fuck" used in any of the posts.

More educated and astute readers will also notice several short vignettes that pop up every few pages under the theme "Funny Tales of Terror." These are each true accounts of frightening things that have happened to me in my life. They first appeared on paper, in a notebook, that was never published. You may also recall the movie based on these stories, where I was portrayed by George Clooney. Or maybe it was Meryl Streep. Now that I think of it, there was no movie.

Some of the names in this book have been changed to protect people who think that they are innocent.

MurMurings

I went to the dentist this morning. He told me that I don't have any cavities. I think my proctologist would strongly disagree.

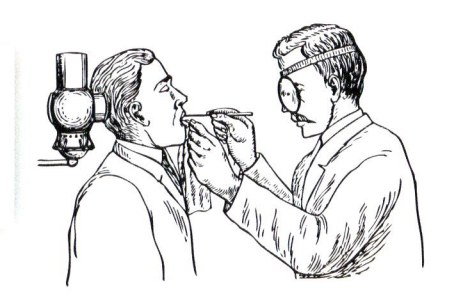

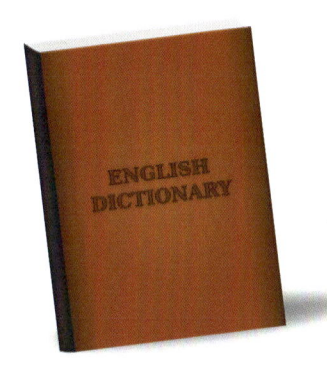

I looked up "idiot" in the dictionary. There were no pictures of anyone. That's what encyclopedias are for.

If you ever witness a crime and don't get a good look at the suspect, you should still give the police a detail like "He had a head." That way, they'll still think you're cooperating.

James Bond movies are so unrealistic. After 25 films, he's killed hundreds of people and bedded dozens of women. But not once has he gotten a call from a telemarketer. I guess this is why men want to be him.

MurMurings

2

Before cameras, were good-looking people considered "paintogenic"?

Did you know...If you remove all of the vowels in your last name it's the same name as your IKEA loveseat?

When Napoleon was being a real jerk, did people say "you have a real You Complex"?

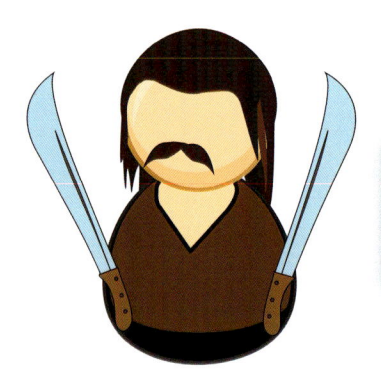

I'm old enough to remember when "getting hacked" meant that you only got chopped up by a machete. Good times.

Whenever I have a bad emergency, I call 9-1-2. They're one better.

We're on it!

MurMurings

3

Simple Social Rules
1. The "beautiful people" never spill anything on their clothes.
2. I just spilled some coffee on my clothes. Again.

Are stir straws jealous of regular straws, or do they just look at them and think "your job sucks"?

Do you think Rembrandt's wife ever had trouble getting him to paint the guest bedroom?

I visited an optometrist after noticing that my vision was getting worse. He asked "do you do 'up close' work? Like look up numbers in a phone book?"

I said "My eyes must be worse than I thought. I haven't seen a phone book since 2004!"

MurMurings

4

My house smells like brownies today. I'm loving that new carpet cleaner. Mmmmmm.

Bwa ha ha

If you see a guy laughing all the way to the bank, don't assume he's rich. He might be going there to settle an overdrawn account. And, he might be laughing because of a really funny childhood memory.

Sometimes, I get inspiration from the most amazing places
But most of the time, I don't.

Smarter than I look

BTW

It takes longer to say "btw" than "by the way".   #worthlessfact

Ice Melter.
Say that three times fast.

MurMurings

5

Have you ever had one of those mornings where you go for a walk, smell your neighbors cooking bacon, and decide to move in with them?

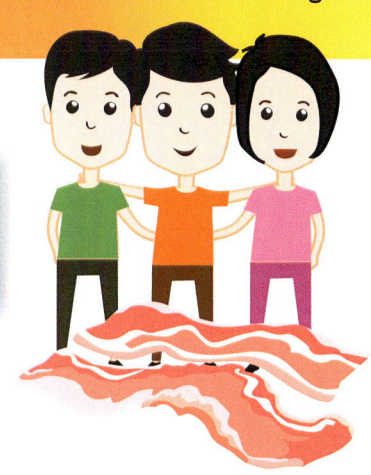

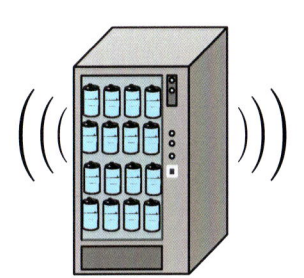

Don't you hate staying in a hotel and the couple in the room next to you is noisily goin' at it all night long...and then, in the morning, you realize that your room is next to the vending machines? Wouldn't expect that from soft drinks!

I broke a mirror a few years ago and had a lengthy period of GOOD luck. WTF is THAT about???

You know you're having a rough day when your face and thumbprint look the same.

MurMurings

I bet it was much easier to get a PhD in Evolution sixteen million years ago than it is today. And cheaper, too.

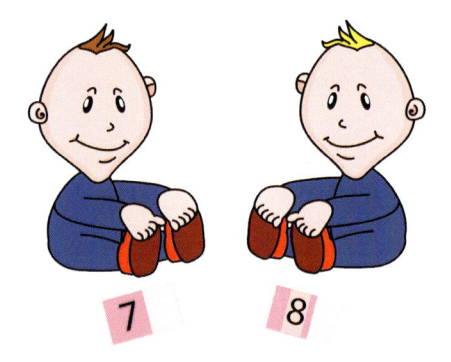

Generally, people don't name their kids after numbers.

The closest I've seen is Sven. And Nate.

I took the Polar Bear Challenge this morning. It was the one where you lay down on your couch like a big ol' lazy polar bear and yawn loudly.

Bring on another challenge.

A friend asked me if I thought he should be a hit man. I said "sure, give it a shot."

Funny Tales of Terror

1. The Time I Almost Got Robbed

Who cannot vividly recall the first time they almost got robbed? That's like forgetting your first real kiss or the time you untangled seven wire hangers without causing damage to your cornea. Big. Life. Moments.

Now, I don't mean getting robbed by paying for a large order of French Fries at Burger King and receiving a medium size portion instead*. I'm talking about the kind of robbery that involves gunplay, knife play, or any other "play" that would inspire someone to hand over their hard-earned cash. And, no, despite being a play, buying tickets for "Hamilton" doesn't count.

In my case, I was about to turn eighteen and was with some friends in a bad part of Baltimore. Imagine a neighborhood where people were so mean they wouldn't even say 'gesundheit' when you sneezed. Or if you spilled gravy on your tie, they wouldn't hand you a napkin. This part of town was even worse.

The five of us ventured into this neighborhood to see a midnight show of a John Waters movie. I suppose that just going to see a John Waters movie was the only omen necessary to tell us that we were in store for a night of danger. But we were as young, restless and bored as horny teens in a Bob Seger song. And as naïve as teens in a Kenny G song. If Kenny G songs had lyrics of course. I don't know why, but something about his soothing soprano sax always conjures up notions of naïve teens to me.

Around 11:30 p.m., we finally found a parking space three blocks away from the theater. Unlike my friends, I had a bad feeling about the potential events that could occur on asphalt between the car and the theater. It was no "Yellow Brick" Road – more like the "See If You Can Find Caked Blood From Last Night's Shooting" Road." If I hadn't been looking upwards and surveying my surroundings, I probably would have easily seen blood. But it only would have allowed me to mention to my friends 'Oh, look. Blood." My intuitive fear increased when I heard the "Theme from 'Jaws'" ominously playing in the background. My friends didn't hear it, probably because it was only in my head and the volume wasn't turned up loud enough. Had I been alone, I would have gotten back in the car and headed for the comfort of my suburban home.

---

*While on that topic, I'm not sure if "Fries" should be capitalized. I've seen it both ways, and 'French fries" looks funny to me.

Nonetheless, we continued walking in the street, with everyone talking, laughing and joking along the way. Except me – I listened tenaciously for howling wolves, screaming banshees, or MBA's locked in trunks screaming for their lives. As we got within a block of the theater, I noticed that two seedy-looking guys emerged from an alley and headed in our direction. It was obvious that if they used shampoo, they did not use conditioner. They smelled like wood pulp and butterscotch. And I was surprised to see that one of them had a terrible hangnail, which was even visible through his glove. At the same time, two more dudes – probably their relatives, judging by the similarity of their frenulums – came around the corner and hustled toward us. I interpreted this as an extreme case of "stranger danger", and concluded that if we walked past the parked cars and onto the sidewalk, the four men could easily close in on us. Within their strategically formed trap, there would be a building on one side, parked cars on the other, and the two groups of men in both "end zones".

And my friends were utterly oblivious to the trap.

"Stay on the street," I warned my friends in a loud whisper. I knew that staying on the street was the only way to avoid being surrounded. "Stay on the street," I pleaded again, in a more urgent tone, seeking safety in numbers. They ignored me.

As if prompted, Michael, the friend about a half-step ahead of the others, walked right onto the sidewalk. The other three followed, leaving me the lone caballero behind in the street like a wet direct mail piece in the rain. Alone and unprotected, I had no choice but to keep up with my friends on the sidewalk. Well, actually, I could have made myself invisible, but that wasn't an option until 1987.

We were descended upon by the four villains like Miss Universe at a clinic that treats priapism.

"Hold on, hold on," said the first guy, blocking the sidewalk. He was an intimidating 5 foot 4 inches tall. Let's call him "Sparky", because "Shorty" is too pejorative. Even though sparks never appeared, I like irony.

"We've got heat," said the guy behind us, pointing to his crotch. I assume that he meant metal guns and wasn't speaking euphemistically. Life Lesson – always assume people are not speaking euphemistically.

Funny Tales of Terror

With the word "heat", we froze. I was seething inside since my friends had ignored my warning. Later, I learned I was seething outside, too. This was an era when seething was a thing. I almost felt compelled to raise my hand and ask if I could be excused since I didn't condone walking on the sidewalk in the first place and thought I should not be subjected to the same fate as my friends.

"Where are you all from?" asked Sparky. He was drinking blue Gatorade. Or windshield washer fluid. Probably Gatorade.

Michael was the richest guy in our group and proud of it. If license plates could hold twenty-three characters his would have read "RICHEST KID IN THE GROUP." Instead, he had to settle for "MR HOWELL" in homage to "Gilligan's Island". He didn't go to school with the rest of us. "Fieldcrest," he replied.

"Good Lord," I thought to myself. "Why don't you just hand over your trust fund certificate and flash him your checkbook? Next time we'll get the Goodyear Blimp to hover over us." With his obtuse behavior, I started to wonder if Michael was a turncoat.

"Fieldcrest," repeated Sparky. "Okay. Perfect. Give us your damn money."

Suddenly, their lookout man hollered from the corner, fifty feet away, "Cops!" Before anyone could reach for their wallet, Sparky and the Jets (the name I gave them in homage to Elton John) ran off in four different directions. We stood there alone, shaking, wondering how close we had come to either being shot, surrendering our money (I had ten dollars), or both. We all silently looked at each other until Michael said to me "don't say I told you so."

"I TOLD you not to walk on the sidewalk," I replied, and walked away. A John Waters movie awaited me. The night was about to get strange.

MurMurings

10

I love the asterisk and its carefree attitude. It's like it is saying "read below. Or not. See if I care." *

I enjoy my coffee with the Sunday paper. But, I like it more with milk and sugar.

I always bring my GPS on an airplane. That way, if the pilots ever get lost or confused, they can ask me for assistance and I can be their little helper.

I love reading a good mystery. Or do I?

I know I could probably Google this, but why bother? Does anyone know if peas are mentioned in the Bible?

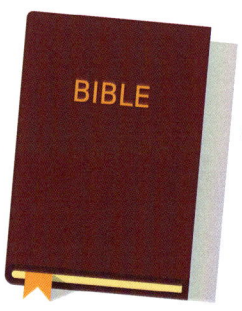

* I don't.

MurMurings

I only have one question about that trick where magicians saw a woman in half.

How do they do that?

I was refused service at Mrs. Fields because of my beliefs. It is my belief that they should give me free cookies. It is their belief that they should not.

I suppose bugs are called bugs because they bug us. But, I prefer to call them schmucks. Because they're schmucks.

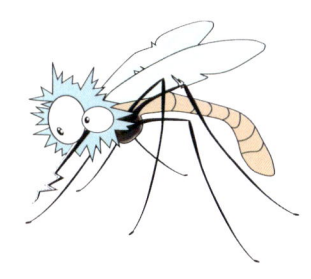

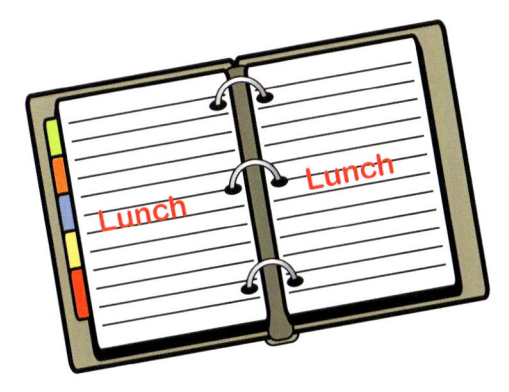

I'll be there for you 23.5/7/364. I need a lunch break and one day off.

I wanted to make a self-deprecating joke but I was too stoopid to think of one.

MurMurings

I would take a bullet for you.
No, wait. Those hurt.
I need a Plan B.

Do jellyfish ever look at other fish and say "funny, you don't look goo-ish"?

In a recent reassessment of the Bible, scholars determined that Adam and Eve wore fig cookies, not fig leaves, as previously believed.

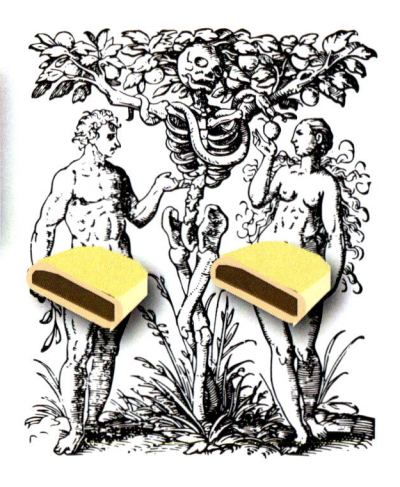

I went fishing with my friend. Because the bait shop was closed.

Most cultures consider cotton candy much tastier than cotton/poly candy.

MurMurings

13

I'm glad life isn't like the movies, where you sneeze once and everyone thinks "yeah, that's it for him."

Sorry!

I'm hoping to finally get that robocall tomorrow with an apology for all of the robocalls I've ever gotten.

I'm not into any of that medieval crap, but you gotta admit, it would be kind of cool to have a shield. Well, maybe not cool, but handy.

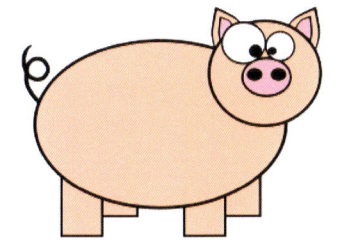

I ate so much last night that my body language is Pig Latin.

MurMurings

I was following a truck that had a pair of plastic novelty testicles (I hope!) hanging from the back. I had to laugh when he made a left turn and coughed.

← COUGHING

My desk chair was really squeaky. So I sprayed the bottom with WD-40. Now my head is a little squeaky. Should have opened a window.

Squeak!!!

Signs you never see.

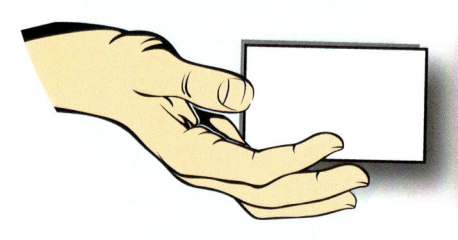

Please Trespass

To save money, my new business cards are blank. I'll leave it up to you to figure out who I am, what I do, and how to reach me.

Funny Tales of Terror

2. When A Dog Bit Me During the 1968 Riots

Sure, I was only seven years old. But, a dog bit me during the April 1968 riots that broke out in Baltimore after the assassination of Dr. Martin Luther King.

April 8, 1968 started like every other Tuesday. As the moon disappeared in the sky, the sun came up. Or it was hidden behind clouds. I can't remember, but it was probably like every other day in that night had reached its inevitable conclusion and people were waking up and doing stuff. I woke up extra early, wiped the sand and seashells out of my eyes, and began to study for my driver's license exam, which was coming up in a little less than ten years. Back then, I was an overachiever – until I hit second grade and the competition got fierce and my dreams were destroyed like pie under a steamroller.

I continued reading until my mother summoned me for breakfast. While some mothers prepared mouthwatering breakfast banquets of eggs, bacon or pancakes, my mom excelled in one area: knowing how much milk, down to the milliliter, to pour into America's most popular cereals. Especially Fruit Loops. It was as if she was a master chef, except for the fact that she couldn't cook. Her recipe for every meal always included a teaspoon of hope.

In school that morning, our teacher Miss Jenkins asked if any of us had a current event that we wished to present to the class. Daryl, who was Vice President of the Paste Eaters Club (and still is), raised his hand and announced that his uncle had been in a car accident the night before.

"Is he alright?" asked Miss Jenkins.

"Mostly," said Daryl. "He broke a bone in his hand."

"Well," replied Miss Jenkins, "that's really not a current event."

"But it happened yesterday," he argued.

"I understand," responded the teacher. "And I'm sure it's sad for him and his family, but it's really not an event of any substance. Something that would be newsworthy. For example, the Martin Luther King shooting…or the curfew in Baltimore City."

Although we lived in Baltimore County, the curfew was still a big deal to us since we were only three blocks from the city line. One girl raised her hand and said "I heard on the news last night that there were snippers on rooftops shooting other people."

"Yeah, and people were breaking into stores and stealing tv sets," added another boy.

"Correct" said Miss Jenkins. "And that's why there's a curfew – the police want everyone off the streets so that nobody gets hurt and no stores get looted."

"What happens if you go outside of your house during the curfew?" I asked.

My teacher looked me directly in the eye and said "you could get arrested. Or maybe even shot."

That thought stayed with me during gym class, when my lack of concentration allowed a kickball to hit me in the head. It stayed embedded in my brain the rest of the school day and even after I got home. The thought, not the kickball. Since the weather was nice (especially the barometric pressure), I went out into the neighborhood to play with some of the other kids my age. We usually congregated at Sharon's house because she had the best swing set and the tallest weeping willow trees.

There were about four or five girls and boys playing by the time I got there at 4:00. Most of the conversation centered around school, the curfew, and The Monkees. Everyone was getting along harmoniously, coasting down the sliding board, swinging on the swings, or just standing still as the earth rotated.

A teenager walked by with his tiny unleashed dog. I don't remember what kind of dog it was, other than small. As I walked toward the sliding board, the dog started running toward me. His owner tried to call him back. "Alfalfa, get back here!"

The dog didn't listen. Or, he listened and just didn't care to stop. Or, maybe he preferred to be called "Al" since "Alfalfa" was too formal. All I know is that he kept running toward me. My only escape route was up the sliding board ladder. My little legs pumped furiously away from the dog directly to the first step. As I lifted my left foot, Alfalfa bit my right leg. It didn't hurt.

Okay, it did hurt.

But not a lot. Not as much as I thought it would. Not as much as when my little sister bit me a few years before that. My dad asked her why she bit me and she said "I didn't bite him. He put his finger in my mouth and my teeth grew." Sounds like something I'd say.

After the first chomp, I was able to get high enough on the ladder so that Alfalfa couldn't reach me. A drop of blood seeped down my leg and directly onto Alfalfa's nose, as his owner got close enough to grab him. Thankfully, he was not mad at me for bleeding on Alfalfa, and he apologized profusely.

"Did he bite you?" he asked me.

"Fuck yeah," I said. Or maybe it was just "Yeah."

"Can I see?"

I rolled up my pant leg and revealed two bloody spots the size of nickels. I think it is safe to say that he freaked out more than I did.

"Does it hurt?" he asked.

"Not too badly," I said. "But I think I better go home."

I walked away from everyone and headed to my house, which was only about two blocks away. I tried not to cry but I must admit that a tear fell from one eye. Not bad for a kid bitten by a dog. When I got home and told my parents what happened, they immediately snapped into action. After cleaning off the wound with rubbing alcohol (didn't hurt), my dad threw me in the car and we went back toward Sharon's house to see if we could locate Alfalfa and his owner.

"We need to see if he has all of his shots," my dad said. "Otherwise, you may need one."

"Getting shots" was not on my schedule for that day, so I was hoping that Alfalfa hadn't ghosted us. Fortunately, Sharon's mother knew who owned the dog and, after a brief phone call, we determined that Alfalfa had, indeed, received all of his shots.

"Well," said my father. "Looks like we should get you to the hospital, just as a precaution. You may need a stitch or two. Let's see what the doctor says."

"Isn't the hospital in the city?" I asked.

"Yes," he said. We were both referring to Sinai Hospital, which was less than three miles away, near Pimlico Race Track. In the city.

"Aren't there curfews there?" I asked.

"Yes," my dad said. "But I really don't think the police will arrest you since you have a medical emergency."

"Will we get shot from a rooftop by snippers?" I asked.

"Snipers," he corrected. "No. That's a different part of the city.

"And we won't get arrested for being out at night?"

"You're obsessing over this," he said.

"What's 'obsessing'?" I asked.

"It's when you worry about something too much," he answered.

"Then, yeah, I'm obsessing," I answered.

"It'll be okay," he said. "The police will take pity on you."

"I hope you're right," I said.

"I just wish that we could have gotten more information about the dog and his owner. For insurance purposes," my dad muttered.

Everything, as far as my dad was concerned, came down to 'for insurance purposes.' One time, after I broke wind loudly at the dinner table, he said "you shouldn't do that. For insurance purposes."

It was an eerie drive from our house to the hospital. Once we crossed over the city line three blocks later, the streets were, indeed, empty. Not a car to be seen. Not even a police presence. Desolation surrounded us, as everyone locked themselves indoors and ate their TV dinners while watching the latest news.

"You sure we're okay?" I asked again.

"Yes, we're safe," he said.

Moments later, we were inside the hospital. All of these years later, I cannot recall the doctor giving me two precautionary stitches, nor do I have a scar. I do, however, remember that he wore a necktie with a hula girl and palm tree motif. Funny how the human brain works. Even funnier how mine does.

In less than an hour, the doctor assured me that I would not turn into a dog and it was time to return home. Once we got into the county again, my dad drove past our house and directly to Baskin-Robbins, where he bought me two scoops of strawberry ice cream. He got a cone with two scoops of chocolate ice cream. I started to take a seat in the store, but he said "Let's get in the car."

We got in and drove toward the city/county line. Five feet away from the imaginary boundary, he pulled over and stopped the car. All we could see in front of us were the empty streets and sidewalks of the city.

We ate our ice cream and my dad put his arm around my shoulder and said "See? Absolutely nothing to be afraid of."

MurMurings

19

If you're going to dig, call Miss Utility. It's the law. Plus, she's kinda cute.

x 2 = ??

I fervently believe that the plural of "stadium" should be "stadiums".

"Stadia" is just bullshit.

Why do they call the little candy bars Fun Size? Where's the "fun" in being consumed with one bite? To me, Fun Size would be about as big as an adult penguin.

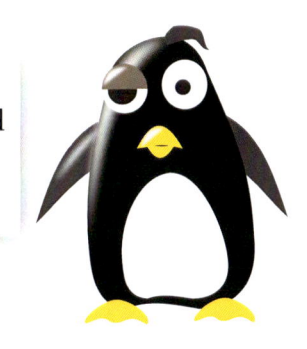

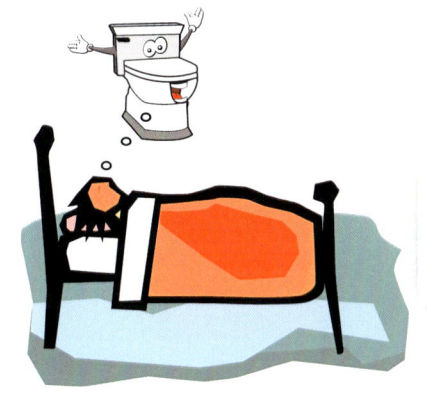

You can be assured that it's time to wake up when you dream that you are asking someone how to find a bathroom.

MurMurings

I forgot to wear my shoes with memory foam. I want my money back.

You know it's cold out when you walk by a clump of mud on the ground and it says "Man, it's cold out."

Seemed to be in a big damn hurry!!!!

MY FREE ADVICE TO MALL SURVEY GATHERERS WITH CLIPBOARDS:

You will acquire more participants if you solicit people LEAVING the restrooms rather than those approaching.

Today's high temp was 43 degrees. I like summer, when I can fry an egg on the sidewalk, instead of fall, when I have to use the damn stove.

To the embarrassed man using the bathroom at Starbucks this morning: They DO have locks on the door. Just saying.

MurMurings

21

I've always had an Open Door Policy. (Note to self: Buy more fly strips.)

I can't figure this out. My face got sunburned at the beach but my feet didn't. My feet are five and a half feet further from the sun. How does this happen?

There are two kinds of dads.

First, the intellectual kind, who reads with his children and helps them with homework.

Then, the kind I saw this morning who hoisted his child up on his shoulders, walked into a store, and hit the kid's face on the top of the door frame.

"You were warned."

I'm thinking about getting a job at night as a sneeze guard.

MurMurings

22

Irony: When workers at a band aid factory go on strike and management has to hire scabs.

How do you pronounce "turmeric"? Is it 'turmeric" or "turmeric"?

My doctor asked me if I ever had hemorrhoid surgery. I told him "Yes, many moons ago."

Is there a drink called "The Lobotomy"? If not, there should be.

Some days life comes at you faster than an announcer listing potential side effects at the end of a medication ad.

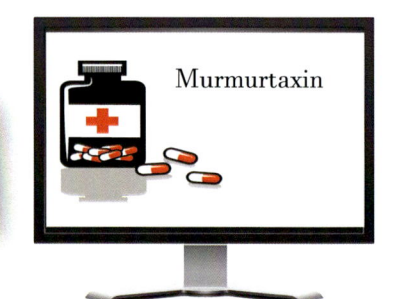

Murmurtaxin

Funny Tales of Terror

3. The First Time I Had Sex

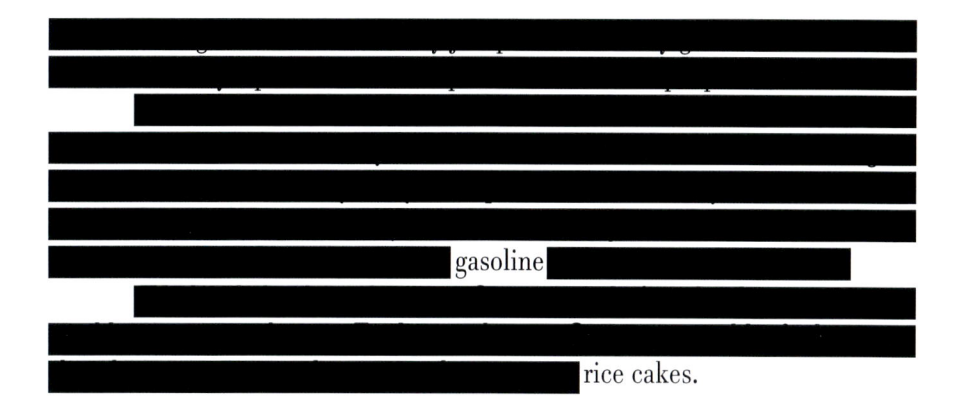

███████████████████████████████████
███████████████████████████████████
███████████████████████████████████
███████████████████████████████████
███████████████████████████████████
███████████████████████████████████
███████████ gasoline ██████████████
███████████████████████████████████
███████████████████████████████████
██████████████████████ rice cakes.

MurMurings

24

The thing I like the most about comfort food is when it looks up at you and asks "Are you comfortable. Is there anything else I can do to make you feel better?"

Are you comfy?

When I was a kid, my allergies were so bad I wasn't even allowed to have a pet peeve.

They say "paper cuts are the worst." Obviously, "they" never got gum-stabbed by a sharp nacho.

My waitress keeps calling me "Boss". Does that mean that I have to give her a tip AND a Christmas bonus?

The man in front of me in line at the grocery store had four items: dried prunes, Metamucil, toilet paper, and a thick novel.
I quickly got the hell away.

MurMurings

25

The phrase "in one ear and out the other" should never be used in relation to a Q-Tip.

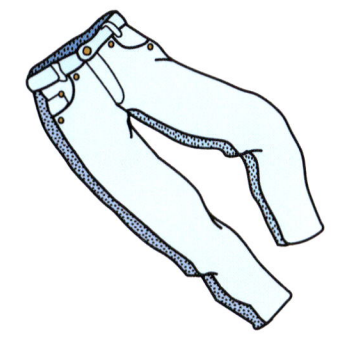

Like everyone else, I put my pants on one leg at a time. Unlike anyone else, it often takes me three or four attempts.

My biggest gripe with the so-called mainstream media is that they have completely ignored the fact that "sassafras" is a very funny word.

Let's be totally honest here. A bowl of cereal is merely soup that won't burn your mouth.

MurMurings

Why are there guys named Guy but no girls named "Girl?"

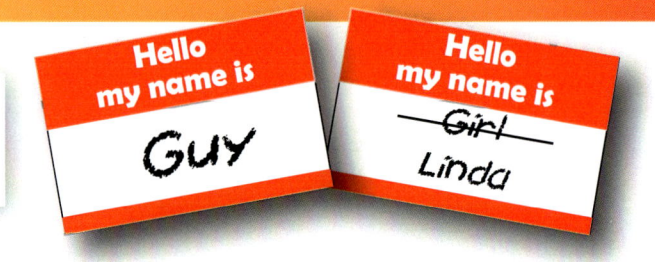

Hello my name is **Guy**

Hello my name is ~~Girl~~ **Linda**

I don't think laughter really is the best medicine, although it can be an extremely effective diuretic.

Have you ever seen someone that looks EXACTLY like you and think "I guess that makes ME the evil twin?"

I remember my dad saying "Don't get smart with me, young man."

I showed him. I got an 8 on my Physics mid-term.

Funny Tales of Terror

4. The Time I Really Got Robbed...While On A Date

Myth: I called my girlfriend and asked where she wanted to go on our date that night. She replied "I don't know. Maybe we can go out and get robbed somewhere."
Reality: She said "Let's go to that comedy club."

About four years after *almost* getting robbed by people who may or may not have had guns, I hit the unlucky jackpot and actually *got* robbed. I know that I should say "spoiler alert", but spoiler alerts are for people who like their closure served to them while blindfolded in a dark room.

It was New Year's Day, 1983. I was on winter break from college when I called Julie in her Maryland apartment from my nearby apartment that afternoon and asked "What do you want to do tonight?"

"Let's go to that comedy club near Georgetown. Garvin's?" she replied from her Maryland apartment. If that sounds familiar, it's because you just read that ten seconds ago. Except for the Georgetown and Garvin's part, which I added since you didn't know the name of the club or where it was located. If none of this sounds familiar, then either your reading comprehension skills are substandard or you're currently driving, texting or preparing lamb kebobs.

I made a reservation for the 8:00 show. Or as they called it, "The Early Show." The show after that was called "The Late Show." It was divinely inspired nomenclature first used by comedy clubs back when Voltaire started touring. I admired it because it caused very little confusion. Unless, of course, they decided to add a third show, in which case I honestly don't know what they would have done.

We decided to have dinner in Georgetown before the show so we would not have to move the car. Finding parking in Georgetown is like finding chocolate ice cream on the sun or a liver spot on a baby. I don't know what prompted me to use those comparisons. Anyway, we finished our dinner at the "Ice Cream and Liver Spot Grill" and left.

Since it was unusually warm for New Year's Day, with lows around fifty degrees, we strolled down M Street, blending in with the large holiday crowd.

While most of the people looked like tourists, some appeared to be locals who had not been home after their New Year's celebrations the night before. Others looked like they had made it home, gone to sleep, awoken in the morning, done things, and then decided to go out again. It was only 7:15, so we decided to walk two miles per hour since we had time. Once or twice, when Julie strolled ahead of me, I tapped her on the shoulder and reminded her "Two miles an hour."

After we walked a few blocks, Julie said that she wanted to see a restaurant on Prospect Street that she had heard was very popular, even though it was closed on New Year's Day.

"It's the place where my niece Trudy lost her dentures,' she said. "I heard it's cool. Maybe we can go there next time we're around here."

I don't know if I was more curious about the restaurant or her niece losing her teeth at a young age. But how could I resist?

Unlike M Street, Prospect Street was poorly lit. It was largely a residential area. Not just any residential area, but home to some of the wealthiest and most influential people in the country. We blended in there like someone with a stiff neck visiting a bobblehead factory. We could see the restaurant about 150 feet away, on the corner. As we walked down the sidewalk holding hands, we passed an alley where a group of young men walked toward us. I probably wouldn't have thought much about it had one of them not said "Let's get 'em."

Do you know that little man who lives in your head and responds to terror simply by proclaiming "Oh shit"? I think his name is Edward, but I'm not sure. Most of the time, he's studying for his finals or preparing lamb kabobs, but at that moment he jumped up out of his recliner and yelled in my ear, from the inside, "Oh shit!" I looked at Julie, who heard the cry of the hunters, and said "Oh, shit" as they drew closer to us. While it would have been very easy for me to run away from them, Julie wore heels that would make it impossible for her to sprint toward safety. Five second later, we were surrounded. Five guys (no relation to the hamburger place) had encircled us. The only way out was to tunnel under them, and neither of us had a shovel or gopher-like superpowers.

Unlike the last gentlemen who were kind enough to attempt to rob me, two of these guys brandished guns. I was unsure if the weapons were Magnums, Berettas or Barnaby Jones since I didn't really know much about guns back then. Kind of like now. But, I did know that they could emit bullets

Funny Tales of Terror

at a rapid enough speed to injure Julie, me, or both of us.

"Give me your money," the shortest one said, pointing his gun at me. The tallest one pointed his gun toward Julie, although he did not aim it directly at her. I raised my arms.

"Give us your money!" hollered another robber. Apparently, the word "please" was not in any of their vocabularies.

I looked at Julie. She put her hands up and nodded a "yes", as if to say "yes, give them the money." She didn't need to make that gesture – the guns were pretty damn persuasive in their own stoic way. I reached into my back pocket and retrieved my wallet. While doing so, my life nearly flashed before me. It started at the moment of my birth and finished the following Tuesday, when I was breast-feeding. I guess I would have needed a much longer robbery experience for it to cycle all the way through. Through it all, they impatiently yelled at me to hurry up. Again, no 'please'. Bastards. As if I was breaking robbery victim etiquette that I should have already known. I suppose the adage is true: you get more with guns than with honey or vinegar. As I presented my wallet, I made eye contact with a driver at the corner stop sign, which was probably another no-no as far as the robbers were concerned.

Since I was twenty-two, I didn't have any credit cards. Just cash. Plus one other important thing. And not what you're thinking. "Take the cash," I said. "But please leave me with my Roy Rogers punch card. I have eight punches on it and with one more I get a free cheeseburger."

The short gunman grabbed the twenty-five dollars I had in my wallet. He tossed the wallet on the sidewalk and they were all gone in an instant. In five different directions. Without a thank you. Nor a fired bullet.

I looked at Julie and said "That was abrupt. I feel like I hardly got to know them."

Julie immediately began to hyperventilate and collapsed in my arms.

"I was so scared," she said as we sat down together. "They were pointing that gun right at your crotch. What if it had gone off?"

"I'm not so sure it didn't," I said. I checked. It hadn't. Before I could answer, a police car pulled up with its siren blaring. Two policemen saw me holding Julie, got out of the car, ran toward us, and asked if we needed help.

"We're okay. We just got robbed!" I said.

"We got a call from one of the neighbors," said the first police officer.

"You must have been the guy with your hands up?"

"Yes," I said. "Was that a smart thing to do?"

"Not really," said the officer.

One day, I'm going to be so much better at getting robbed.

"Is she okay?" asked the second policeman.

"I'm just shaking a little," said Julie.

"Where did they go?" asked the policeman.

"They took twenty-five dollars and went in five different directions," I said. "Basically, they each got five dollars. I'm guessing they went to buy a few pizzas."

"And they were armed?"

"Yes, definitely," said Julie.

Before they could ask another question, a second police car pulled up. One of the suspects was in the back seat. The policeman got out of the car and asked if we could identify his passenger as one of the perpetrators. We looked at him and confirmed that he had pulled a gun on us.

"How did you catch him so fast?" Julie asked.

"Criminals are basically morons, and this one is no different," he replied. "He made it easy. We heard the robbery call on our radio and he was standing on the corner, about fifty feet away, nervously looking at us. I stared him down. He froze in place and finally said to me 'I'm not who you're looking for. I didn't rob anyone.' I said to him 'I never said you did…now get in the car.' And here we are."

"Mensa member, obviously," I said.

The first responders asked us to get into their car so we could talk privately. We sat in the back seat and a few seconds later the driver yelled "close the door! The others were spotted near the canal!"

We immediately shut the door and began speeding through the narrow streets of Georgetown at 85 miles per hour. Each bump threw us into each other as the sirens blared and we saw people moving out of the way. Except for the fact that it was terrifying, the ride was damn fun. I even suggested that they charge people twenty dollars for a ride like this (thirty with a boxed lunch). Moments later, the cruiser stopped along the canal, several blocks away from all retail. It was dark and silent as the cops jumped out of the car and told us not to go anywhere during their pursuit.

Funny Tales of Terror

We huddled together, completely in shock from what had occurred over the last five minutes. Finally, Julie said what I was thinking. "So, we're alone and unarmed in an abandoned police car and they think that the robbers are in this general vicinity. Any chance said robbers could come back here to silence us?"

"If five guys are stupid enough to steal twenty-five bucks," I said, "then they're stupid enough to do anything."

Not the answer that Julie was looking for. Even if it was the right answer.

We sat there for what seemed like an hour (it was six minutes), tapping our toes to the rhythm of each other's heartbeat. I remember thinking "this could make a great story one day – maybe as part of an anthology." Finally, the policemen got back into the car and announced "No luck."

The next stop was D.C. Police Headquarters, where detectives took a formal statement from us. While my recollection may be a little fuzzy, I think we were in the same building where they used to film episodes of "Barney Miller" and possibly "Laverne & Shirley". Detective Snow kindly greeted us, took us into his office, and asked generic questions.

"How many were there?" Hundreds, I thought.

"What did they look like?" Spoiled potato salad.

"Did they hurt you?" Yes. They were impolite and impatient.

This continued for about twenty minutes, with the detective telepathically reading my thought bubbles and then furiously typing them out. I wish I knew how he did that. I guess it was just police intuition. After his last query, he said "Okay, I've got your statements. If this goes to trial, you'll be called in to testify. Now, do you have any questions?"

"Yes," I said. "If you drink Dr. Pepper and get sick, can you sue for malpractice?"

"Not my area," he replied.

It was still worth asking, I thought.

When we were permitted to leave, we decided we should still go to Garvin's comedy club. We weren't going to let hundreds of robbers spoil our plans for the evening. Even if we had no cash and would have to wash dishes, wipe up up dirty jokes from the floor, or do whatever else comedy clubs normally deemed as suitable forms of payment.

EPILOGUE

This section did not have to be an epilogue, but I always wanted to write one when I was a child. Instead, my parents made me sit on top of metal trashcans so they wouldn't blow away.

Two months after the robbery, Julie and I were called to testify at a grand jury hearing. We learned that just before the robbery, the five thieves tried to steal a pizza from a delivery guy. After the robbery, they took their booty, minus the five dollars from their captured compadre, went into a shop and bought a pizza.

Mensa, indeed. With some pepperoni and extra cheese.

MurMurings

33

Acceptable: When you have to speak publicly and, to relax, you imagine the audience is naked.

Unacceptable: When you imagine the same naked audience following you to your car.

Does a banana a day keep the urologist away?

On July 5th, you know your neighbors weren't being safe with their fireworks when you look at your lawn in the morning and find a thumb and a testicle.

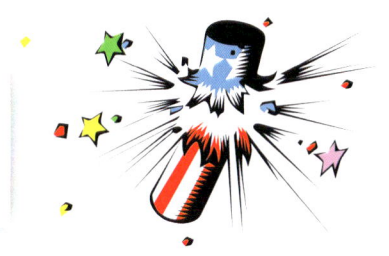

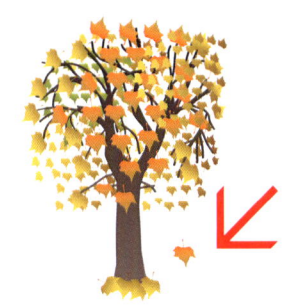

A Poem:
Leaves falling.
They touch the ground.
I am not a poet.

On this date in 1937, the Supreme Court ruled that the hanging wedgie was illegal. The decision was met with a loud cheer from dweebs and dorks everywhere.

There is only one thing worse than when your toilet paper rolls into the next stall and you have to ask the occupant for a little help...and that's finding out that there is no one in the next stall.

What the hell is that? →

When I read a used book and find a coffee stain in it, I silently pray that it's a coffee stain.

When I was 13, I wrote a letter to myself that was not to be opened until January 2021.
I finally opened it.
It said "throw away the milk. It expired."
I always was wise beyond my years.

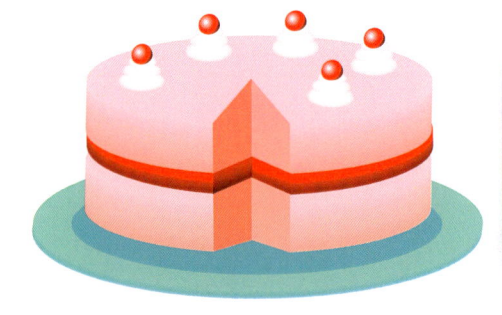

Lumpy Milk

You can't have your cake and eat it too...unless you don't fill up on bread and you only have a small salad for dinner. Then it's okay.

Funny Tales of Terror

5. My first car accident

It doesn't take much talent or determination to get your driver's license when you're sixteen. But, it does require special skills to get into an accident a mere eighty-four minutes after receiving that driver's license.

Triumph and shame each paid me a visit that afternoon. And now, of course, human nature dictates that I remember nothing about the triumph and everything about the shame.

I received my driver's license on October 23, 1977. It was a sunny afternoon. I wore argyle socks. Two of them. This is all I remember about receiving the actual license.

However, on my way home from the License Giving Place (Department of Motor Vehicles? Like I said, I don't remember much about that part), I stopped at my friend Jacob's house to show off my proud achievement. We sat on his porch and talked for about ten minutes and then I told him I needed to go home and do my homework. It is important to note that Jacob lived on a street that curved. My friend Gabe lived on a street that didn't curve, but that's not important. Unless you're Gabe, who was famous for bragging about his perfectly straight street. Gabe later became a Geometry teacher. Anyway, I walked from Jacob's porch to my mom's Impala, got in, and fired up the engine. I checked my side view mirror, saw nothing, and slowly pulled out.

Impact happened quickly. An elderly woman had rapidly come around the curve and my front left bumper hit her passenger side door. Damn, how I wished I had visited Gabe instead! While it was not, by any means, a bad accident, the grinding sound of metal on metal was enough to make the hairs on the back of my neck stand up and want to run away with the circus. To this day, I'm convinced that a handful of them became clowns, two more trained tigers, and another dozen formed a trapeze act. The hairs that stayed with me followed my head and the rest of my body as we all got out of the car to face our fate.

When you get into an accident, even a minor fender bender, every man, woman, child and gopher within the sound of the collision immediately descend upon you. Miraculously, in the twenty seconds from the time the accident occurred until I got out of my car to speak to the woman, there were seventeen hundred bystanders on this quiet suburban street. At least, it sure seemed that way. Later, I found out that there were eight. And one of them was there because she thought she heard the Good Humor Man. Nonetheless, they all held up their phones, which was odd because it was 1977 and they were corded phones. Maybe they were on to something.

My heart pounded as I approached the other driver whose car was still in the middle of the quiet street. By my estimation, she was old enough to date Yul Brynner's grandfather. She showed no visible signs of injury, other than a few wrinkles on her face that were probably there before. If she was upset, she hid it well. Something told me she had experienced her fair share of accidents.

I immediately apologized and said that I didn't see her coming around the curve. Since there was a small dent on her passenger's door, we exchanged phone numbers and driver's licenses.

"Your driver's license still smells of laminate," she noted. "When did you get it?"

I looked at my watch and said "Eighty-four minutes ago."

She smiled and said "I don't know what to say." Quite a few people have said that to me in my lifetime.

She told me that she would take the car to her body shop and let me know how much the repair would cost. If you ever are fortunate enough to be in a small crash, I hope your crash-mate is as sweet as Mrs. Kravitz. She was very nice and also had the uncanny ability to detect the smell of laminate.

When I got home and told my parents what had happened, they took it surprisingly well. My mother told me to wash the car and, when I was finished, she ran me over with it.

MurMurings

37

The strangest thing happened to me this morning.
I met myself from the future.
At breakfast. We got along fine... until it was time to pay the check.

"What's that?" I asked the guy in the health store, while pointing to a bottle.
"It's for skin," he said.
"Is that one word or two?" I asked.

Tomorrow will be hotter or colder, depending on the weather.

When life gives you lemons, sell them. Even in a buyers' market, you'll make a 100% profit, and that's pretty darn good.

38 MurMurings

There's no business like show business. Although I do hear about some amazing things from the tire industry.

If want to make people smile when you're taking their picture, you can tell them to say "sneeze". Because that works too.
Unless, of course, they sneeze.

Words?

When you have a heated discussion with someone, it's called "having words". But don't all conversations have words? Someone really dropped the ball when inventing that phrase.

If the police could shoot radar to determine how fast your mind is going, I think a lot of people would register well below the speed limit.

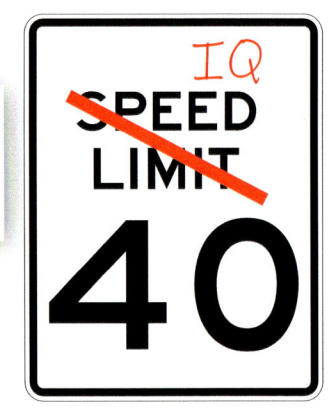

MurMurings

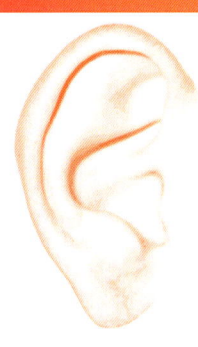

I held a conch shell to my ear on the beach and I could hear the ocean.
Then, I held a water bottle to my ear and I could hear the ocean.
Finally, I held a pillow to my ear...and could still hear the ocean.
This could simply be a hearing problem.

It's a proven fact that lies make your pants catch on fire and money can burn a hole in your pocket.
So, I'm investing in a company that makes asbestos pants.

Before smart phones, the most competitive members of society actually left bars and went to the library to settle their arguments.

Aretha Franklin visits an optometrist.
Doctor: Please read the top line.
Aretha: R-E-S-P-E-C-T
Doctor: Next line?
Aretha: R-E-S-P-E-C-T
Doctor: Your vision isn't very good.

J V T D
L Y M R
H N P Q Z K
E D C F O R T
C D T F E P Z R
P E T O Z C L D

The next time you wake up really tired in the morning, pour coffee in your iron. You may still be tired but your clothes will get you through the day.

MurMurings

I looked at my neighbor's house and hollered to him "You have huge icicles."
He thanked me, which made me realize he may have thought I said something else.

Do you think people would watch a TV show about shoppers trying to find the best possible deal on root beer?

Do women named Lola laugh out loud more than other people?

I formed a new band that plays jazz-infused songs about pastries. We're called Steely Danish.

I never hit the snooze button. Because I don't want to lose.

Funny Tales of Terror

6. The time I nearly got struck by lightning

      I vividly remember the day that my wife Karen and I nearly got hit by lightning. It was July 6th, 2017. If we HAD actually received a direct lightning strike, I probably would have remembered it as July 43, 1538.

      Karen and I were on the beach in our favorite resort town of Nags Head, North Carolina. We were comfortably situated on reclining beach chairs about six miles from Kitty Hawk, where the Wright Brothers are credited with inventing flight. Orville and Wilbur, not their other two brothers, Otis and Reuchlin, or any other combination of the four brothers. * Can you imagine the indignity of being Wright Brothers, but not THE Wright Brothers? Anyway, it was a cloudy afternoon, moderately humid, around eighty degrees. Pleasant beach weather, with occasional cool breezes that licked the sweat off of your skin and then moaned "blecch."

      There was a large population of jellyfish assembled near the shoreline that afternoon, similar to the Allies in their Higgins Boats on the morning of D-Day, just before the invasion began. I recalled the time when, early in our marriage, Karen had been swimming in the ocean one morning and suddenly found herself surrounded by a school of jellyfish. Judging by their individual sizes, it was probably a high school or institution of advanced learning. Karen miraculously ran across the surface of the water, a feat I had only witnessed in a Tom & Jerry cartoon. Afterwards, she vowed never to go in the ocean if jellyfish were visible. Even if it was one jellyfish, only seen with binoculars. Because he could be a spotter.

      Instead of swimming, we kept our noses buried in our novels that afternoon. A nearby family made a sand sculpture depicting unfair labor practices in the early twentieth century. I never got a good look at it, but I think they were focusing on Chicago. Another family buried their grandmother in the sand. I would have preferred that they had done so in a cemetery, but some people are less self-conscious than others.

---

* There were actually several more brothers. I think they were Dopey, Sneezy and Bashful, but I can never remember. There were also sisters. Just read David McCullough's book on the Wright Brothers and you'll learn everything you need to know about their family, airplanes, and Cher.

During our afternoon reading/sunbathing/sweating session, I managed to fall asleep. Often, when I fall asleep while reading a book, I vividly dream that I am still reading. But the book ends up going in some odd directions. Most memorable to me was the time when a John Grisham novel had a chapter that took place in Middle Earth and Tess of the d'Urbervilles appeared out of nowhere, posting selfies on Facebook. Until Huckleberry Finn told her to stop. Occasionally, the dreams are even odder.

Karen also dozed off for close to an hour that fateful afternoon, her back to the ocean, her toes embedded in the sand. When she awoke, she tapped my shoulder and said "those clouds from the west are looking kind of mean."

"'Steal your lunch money and pants' mean?" I asked. "Or 'decapitate you with a machete' mean?"

"Worse," she said. "Look."

"Look" is always good advice. In this case, it paid off. As advertised, the clouds to the west were as dark as the burnt oatmeal my mom used to serve for breakfast. I checked the weather app on my phone. It reported thunderstorms about six miles away.

"Let's pack up and call it a day," I replied.

Just as I was pronouncing the 'a' or 'y' in 'day', a large blinding bolt of lightning struck down on the beach, about 150 feet away. I would say "it came out of nowhere", but clearly it originated in the sky.

We each felt the force of this explosive, mighty power on the top of our heads. It was like someone had placed a large wooden plank upon our craniums and jumped on it. Our mouths got tingly and our saliva had an electric taste, like when Mountain Dew goes bad. From this experience, I can also report that, when you are in that close proximity to a lightning strike, your hair really does stand on end. And not just the hair on your head. It's the hair everywhere, including places where you did not have hair when you were seven years old. Probably even the hair sitting on the floor at the salon where you got your last cut, too.

We looked at each other with wild eyes, each wondering for a moment if we were still alive. True to the cliché, my life had flashed before me, although the audio part was garbled while the video portion was quite vivid.

Then, we broke our own land speed record for tossing towels in our bag, disabling the umbrella, and folding our chairs. The entire operation took

Funny Tales of Terror

ten seconds, give or take nine seconds. Since the lightning strike was to the north, we ran south across the beach so we could gain shelter from a second strike. Because lightning can strike twice. Just look at Golden Earring, who managed to get a second, bigger hit after "Radar Love".

We ran past a couple who were actually about fifty feet farther from the lightning strike than we were. The man, seemingly in his early forties, repeatedly hollered to no one in particular "I just got hit by lightning! I just got hit by lightning! I just got hit by lightning."

"No, you didn't," I said. "You'd be dead if you did!"

"I just came close to getting hit by lightning!" he hollered, correcting his inaccurate assessment. I felt like I had done my good deed for the day. "I just came close to getting hit by lightning," he repeated several more times. It didn't have the same cadence as his original claim, but I'm sure it made him feel important. Just because I was in the south doesn't mean he was a southerner. But, regardless of his birthplace, it's safe to say he was a moron.

Out of breath from running about seventy yards on the sand, we finally got to an oversized gazebo just as the rains came down. We had survived the lightning strike, even if we had minor headaches and temporary difficulty counting by eights. We had withstood the worst that nature had to offer us and managed to defiantly survive it. We had tasted electricity, felt the concussion on our heads, and maintained continence. We felt invincible, capable of defying death and laughing at danger.

So, later that night, I took a shower with a plugged-in toaster. And, as you can see, I'm absolutely fine. Except I can only name four Wright Brothers or Dwarves at any given time.

MurMurings

44

When life gives you beans, make beanade.

Kidney stones are not your friend. I don't have them, I'm just telling you to watch your back.

Mmmm... kiwi.

Imagine a world where ALL books are "scratch and sniff." Even math textbooks. Just ponder that a moment.

If you think it's hard to detect sarcasm on Facebook, try figuring it out in Morse Code.

MurMurings

45

MAY 1

May 1 is April Fools' Day for procrastinators.

Beerundipity: When your waiter brings you a beer that you didn't order.

Is it funny to see someone hit oneself in the face while opening a beach umbrella?
Yes.
But is it funnier the second time?
Again, yes.

Restaurant Rule of Thumb: Whenever you have to badly use the bathroom and you're locked out, it's ALWAYS the busboy.

MurMurings

Little known trivia:
St. Patrick's last name was Greenblatt.

Is a good humorist someone who is funny or someone who sells ice cream?

At some point in history, physicians decided that if you were subjected to medical tests and the results were in your favor, it would be deemed "negative". And, if they were against you, they were "positive".

I'm guessing that after this decision was made, the physicians forgot to say "We're just effing with you all! Let's do it the other way!"

I've got some very negative news for you.

I met a guy named Lumpy and accidentally called him Bumpy. He was offended. My question is this: how can someone named Lumpy be offended at being called Bumpy?

MurMurings

The Tupperware Convention and a conference for new moms are both in town today.
No wonder people are trying to burp me.

I had an emergency appendectomy in 1982. At the time, I was told I'd never miss my appendix. But sometimes, especially around the holidays, I miss it terribly.

I always thought that "The Ten Commandments" was a good movie, but it would have better if they had freeze-framed on every character in the end and said where they are now.

Do psychics have Secret Santas?

MurMurings

48

If I ever wanted to overhear two people talking, I wouldn't want to be a "fly on the wall". I'd rather be a ceiling fan. Because no one ever tries to kill a ceiling fan.

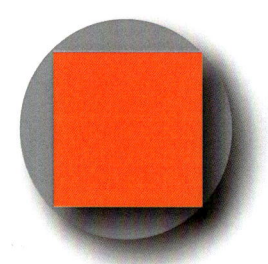

I just put a square peg in a round hole. What do I win?

Just once, I'd like to hear a phone tree message that says "Don't worry, you don't need to pay close attention...In our company history, we have NEVER changed our information or extensions...oh, and, Mr. Siegel, my oh my, you sure are handsome."

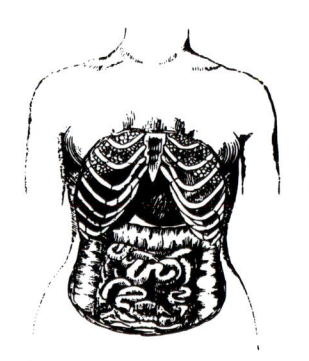

If you eat a meal that sticks to your ribs, I beg you! Please see a doctor!

Is it okay for birds to eat sesame seeds that fall off of a bagel? Asking for a bird that can't type.

Funny Tales of Terror

7. My Kingdom for a Rest Stop

The conflict presented in most landmark works of literature can often be reduced to the simplest of struggles, like "Man vs. Machine, "Man vs. Man", "Man vs. Animal' or "Man vs. Nature", to name a few.

This is a story of "Man vs. Coffee and Bran." While this could certainly happen to a woman, I use the "proverbial" man since I'm a man, I'm proverbial at times, and it happened to me. I don't think I owe you much of an explanation beyond that.

In the early spring of 1992, my wife Karen and I awoke in a hotel in Wilkes-Barre, Pennsylvania. This was not a surprise to us, since we had gone to sleep in the same hotel the night before. We had previously selected this small town as our stopping point for our road trip from Maryland to Cooperstown, New York, where we were going to visit the Baseball Hall of Fame. Time permitting, we were also going to visit a Holstein cow we once saw on a postcard.

For those who have never been to Wilkes-Barre, I'm pretty sure this is where John Wilkes Booth and Chuck Barre wrote 'Sweet Little Sixteen".

When the 6:30 wake up call came, I was as excited as a (gentile) kid on Christmas Day. I had gone to the Hall of Fame twenty years before, with my family, but this was different because I had accumulated a vast knowledge of baseball since my last visit. This time, when I saw Tris Speaker's skull from his childhood, it would mean something to me.

Karen was less excited. Not indifferent, just less excited. Although she wouldn't admit it, I think she had already seen Tris Speaker's skull. Anyway, we opened the curtains in the hotel room and saw snowflakes falling onto the parking lot. They were big – about the size of an infant's thumb. And just as wet. Recognizing the need to get on the road quickly, we packed, checked out, and loaded the car.

Knowing that we had about a three-hour drive ahead, I took advantage of the free coffee and muffins in the hotel lobby. There was a mother with her little boy sitting nearby. For some reason, the lad was wearing a fedora. He eyeballed me closely and cracked his knuckles. Then he called his mother a dame. I waited for him to light a match on the wall, but he never did.

Karen and I went out to our Subaru and I cleaned off the snow with my my two ungloved hands.

"It's damn cold out here," I said. "All twenty-one digits agree."

We pulled out of the hotel parking lot and the snowflakes had increased to the size of an infant's thumb plus one finger. Traffic was light in anticipation of the dangerous road conditions; I surmise that schools were already delayed or canceled. The asphalt looked only lightly salted, particularly when compared to a potato chip. I don't know why the salt trucks weren't out in full force yet. I'm still waiting for answers from the mayor.

Moments later, we were heading north toward New York on I-83. At first, the conditions were moderate since the road had not yet frozen. Then, as the roads got worse, we saw many cars blow by us in the left lane at unsafe speeds. As if that wasn't bad enough, one driver was shaving and another seemed to be taking air guitar lessons.

About twenty minutes later, we saw several cars that had unsafely passed us either neatly arranged in ditches or against the guard railing. Neither of us made fun of these bold, stupid drivers. Actually, now that I recall, we laughed hysterically, offered up jokes about their mothers and grandmothers, and listened to a mix tape called "Music to Flip Your Car By", a compilation of tunes all about people driving in bad conditions.

And then the coffee and bran muffin kicked in.

Was it karma? Or, worse - carma? For a complete medical explanation of what happens when coffee and bran interact within the confines of a human body, please refer to the appendix in the back of the book. Or to the area near your appendix in your abdominal region.)

"My stomach feels a little gurgly" I announced. As if making an announcement like that, in the middle of nowhere, would summon the magical bathroom fairy who would tele-transport me to a bathroom.

"I can't hear you," Karen said. "Your stomach gurgled too loud."

Needless to say, the Magical Bathroom Fairy did not arrive. She was probably taking a snow day.

So there we were, in two inches of snow on the highway, with:
- No signs indicating the nearest exit.
- No rest stops.
- No trees.
- An explosive device (me) in the car.

Funny Tales of Terror

An overwhelming, all-consuming feeling of helplessness and panic set in. To say that my forehead was clammy is an understatement.

"You have clams head," Karen observed. Not clam. Clams. Until the front changed and it went from clammy to rainforest.

We needed to get somewhere FAST, but the icy conditions prevented us from reaching the speed limit. While I knew that something as innocuous as a fender bender would have alleviated my problem, it was far from the desired solution that I was seeking.

The next five minutes seemed like fifteen hours. I started reciting the Gettysburg Address over and over in my head, just to take my mind off of the situation at hand. My guts began singing the lyrics to 'Blowing in the Wind", which was probably not the best selection at that moment. I could feel long spears, the kind held by the natives in the old Tarzan movies, as they entered my body all along my GI tract. I wondered how much longer I could hold on.

And then, like a godsend from Ronald McDonald and all things holy, we saw a sign that said "McDonald's – Next Exit. 1.5 miles."

Hope. At last.

We exited the interstate and turned west. No trace of McDonald's. I accused the highway sign of mocking me. I used language that would have shocked a seasoned prison guard. We continued for another minute - which seemed like forty-three and half minutes - until the famous bathroom/restaurant finally appeared just past a curve. I drove into the parking lot at the speed of a compromised digestive system. In what seemed like one motion, I stopped the car, got out, and ran to the door. All the while hoping that the bathroom was not occupied, as I had no more reserves left in my delicate situation.

At that point, I invented - and later patented - a new dance that no human had seen before as I gravitated toward the door. It was not pretty. And neither was the last obstacle. Some idiot left his German Shepard leashed to a railing by the front door. The dog barked at me, his teeth revealing how displeased he was by his incarceration. "Man vs. Animal" co-aligned against "Man vs. Coffee and Bran." The moment of truth, featuring a soundtrack with a growling dog and a growling stomach. There could only be one winner. Either get bitten by the dog or morbidly embarrass myself.

When you have a burst of adrenalin and a desire to maintain a bottom feeder level of human dignity, amazing things can happen. In this case, since I had a running start, I was able to jump completely over the dog and gain entry into the promised land. I even did a clean flip just before I touched terra firma. Emphasis on "clean".

Mission accomplished.

I returned to the car and Karen asked "Do you realize you nearly single-handedly converted that McDonald's into a drive-thru?"

"Yes," I said. "But it would have been worth the lawsuit."

The things we endure, just to see Tris Speaker's brains.

MurMurings 53

If you decide to lead a horse to water, make damn sure it's a thirsty horse. Otherwise, don't even bother.

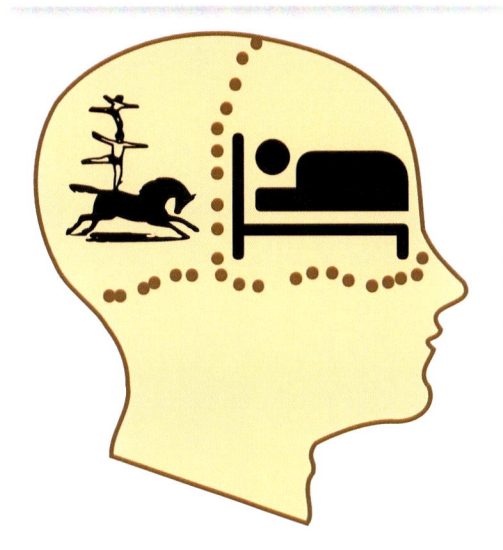

I've got a lot going on in the back of my mind. It's the front and middle that are mostly vacant.

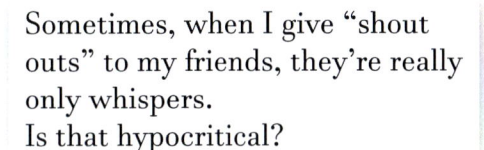

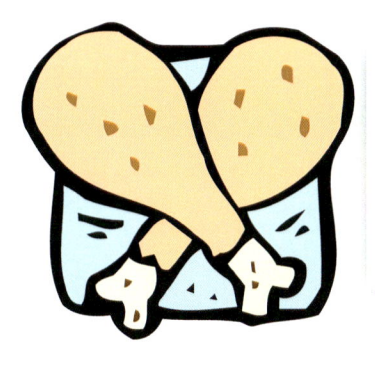

Sometimes, when I give "shout outs" to my friends, they're really only whispers.
Is that hypocritical?

ANTI NOISE

I watched a family of five at a table in Panera. Dad was eating a salad and everyone else had chicken they carried out from KFC. To me, that's like going to a church and praying in Hebrew.

MurMurings

It took me three hours to install my new garbage disposal. When I finally crawled out from under the kitchen sink, it reminded me of that time when my mom birthed me.

At some point, someone in charge said "gubernatorial" instead of "governatorial". And I don't even know who to thank for introducing such a funny word.

I saw a shopping bag slowly blow down the street. It wasn't a big deal, except that it waited to cross at a crosswalk in busy traffic. Smartest. Bag. Ever!

My valuable life lesson to you:
This morning, my "Check Tire Pressure" light went on.
Rather than procrastinating,
I immediately pulled into the closest shopping center, bought a band-aid, and covered the light.
You're welcome.

Do you realize how many less posts there would be on Facebook if it had a breathalyzer?

MurMurings 55

Spotify just informed me that one of my instrumental jazz songs is "explicit". Even with my vivid imagination, I can't figure out how.

Today, I saw two butterflies frolicking together. It made me wonder how long they knew each other.

What is WRONG with people??? Folks in the mall get so mad at me when I say "feel how cold my fingers are" and touch their faces.

Our society is crumbling.

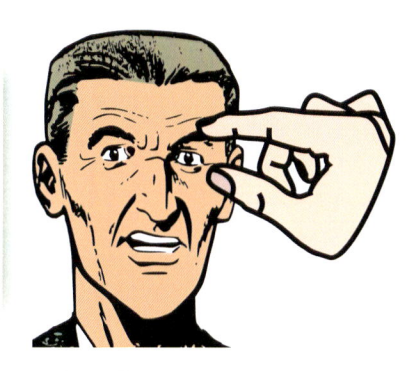

I got a friend request on Facebook from someone who owns a candy factory. I almost accepted it because, well, candy. Yay! Then I remembered what my parents taught me about strangers with candy.

Overheard at the supermarket today: "Honey, go down Aisle Six and get some toast."

Again, our society is crumbling.

MurMurings

Be kind to people.

If you have to throw someone under the bus, at least make sure it's in park.

I heard a radio ad for a place that announced "It's our 20th anniversary. Free coffee and doughnuts for everyone all day."

As it turns out, they only meant everyone that goes to their store.

How did Saint Joseph get stuck with children's aspirin? Was he too immature for all of the responsibilities associated with adult aspirin?

Pull my finger

I bet that even the captain of the Chess Team at the School of Hard Knocks is a pretty tough dude.

Funny Tales of Terror

8. Bomb Scary

It was a dark and stormy night, except for the fact that it was a sunny afternoon in May. I was sitting at my office desk, minding someone else's business, when I suddenly remembered I had a question for our HR Director. Usually, I only have one question a year and, typically, it's "What does HR stand for again?"

This time, my question was more complex. Earlier in the month, I had been told that all senior managers, including me, had to complete an online course in office emergency preparedness. It was a new requirement from our company's insurance provider, a directive that was as popular as an ice cream shop in a vacant Alaskan shopping mall. Once again, my father was right. Everything is done for insurance purposes.

I had badly procrastinated the completion of this assignment and knew that the deadline was hanging over my head like decaying mistletoe in spring. While the thought of watching training videos with people choking on root beer or bleeding out from tiger bites had morbid appeal, I had been solidly busy with work projects during the month. Being forced to watch eight hours of office injury porn on top of my regular responsibilities reminded me of the time I told my English Lit professor "You know, we DO have other classes?" To which she replied "And I have other students." Even with a Logic Flow Diagram, I could not discern what that meant. Which is why I skipped James Joyce's "Ulysses" that weekend and read the comic book version.

I walked thirty feet down the hall and into the HR Director's corner office. Then I knocked on the door. I probably need a little guidance with room-entering rules of engagement, now that I think about it. Maybe that would be covered in one of the training films.

Karla, the HR Director, was sitting behind a desk covered in piles of papers or their more elegant cousins – manilla folders filled with papers. She looked up at me with a forced smile, and at that point I remembered that an HR Director is the person responsible for getting paper cuts so that none of the other employees have to. In most companies, it's also the person who says "It's the twenty-first century. Can't we go paperless?"

"You busy?" I asked.

"No," she said. "I was just about to file my snails."

"Nails?" I asked.

"Yes. I meant nails. Damn auto-correct."

And then I asked my question. "When do I have to complete the damn emergency preparedness training?"

"The final exam is tomorrow," she said.

"That's what I was afraid of," I replied.

Before I could say another word, we felt the floor violently shake, heard a loud explosion, and watched Karla's windows crack and then blow inward. I heard a woman scream and realized that it was me. We looked at each other, completely baffled by what had just occurred. Was it a terrorist attack? Did the air conditioning unit on top of the building blow up? Did the fast food joint across the street serve that day-old mystery "food" from the bottom of the bin?

"Holy shit!" exclaimed Karla.

"Holy shit!" I replied.

In my lifetime, shit has never been holier than at that moment. But that ordained moment, filled with silence and confusion, did not last very long.

Within seconds, all forty of our co-workers started hustling down the carpeted hallway and past us toward the building's side door. Karla and I followed them outside where the source of the explosion was partially revealed. A billowing black mushroom cloud, about the size of three football fields (if you include the parking lots and outer perimeter of vendors selling knock-off jerseys), rapidly expanded above us. It was coming from the train tracks about two hundred yards behind the building.

I soon learned that a garbage truck driver had maneuvered past the lowered crossing gate and smashed into an oncoming freight train ten minutes before the actual explosion. The train had derailed and spilled volatile chemicals on the grass. Whereas peanut butter mixed with chocolate (alias "Reese's Peanut Butter Cup") is a tasty treat, commingling every chemical from the Periodic Table of Elements can, and did, have disastrous results. Minutes after the accident, once the chemicals in the soup exchanged pleasantries, they essentially formed a bomb that had no other choice but to detonate.

Or, in layman's terms, BOOM!

In a chemist's terms, KABOOM! (My father was a chemist, so I guess you could say I have chemicals in my blood. That's how I know for certain that KABOOM is the correct term. Then again, I could be wrong.)

Funny Tales of Terror

Standing outside, surrounded by co-workers, I realized that if there was one violent explosion, there could be more. I call this the Oreo Theory of Big Bangs, although in some scientific journals I've also referred to it as the Nacho Chips Theory of Big Bangs. In either dictum, one is never enough. Either way, I knew that this train reaction could have a chain reaction. And these reactions could be even more powerful and dangerous.

As my heart pounded to an unusual disco/funk/punk/ gospel/bluegrass beat, I determined that my safest action would be to get in my car and drive as far away as possible.

At that point I realized that my car keys were on my desk. Assuming, of course, I still had something resembling a desk.

They say that firemen that run into a building when everyone else is running out are among the bravest people on earth. So, even though I was the idiot who left his keys on his desk, I got to feel what it is like to run into a building when everyone else is running out. In short, it's not a good feeling. Particularly when you get shmooshed into a wall, your feet get trampled upon, or you get a wedgie. To this day, I'm less concerned about who gave me the wedgie and more focused on why. Despite feeling like a salmon swimming upstream, I was able to get to my office, grab my keys, and head to my car.

Still shaking profusely, I drove across a six-lane road and momentarily parked at Taco Bell so that I could gather my thoughts and maybe get a good selfie with a genuine photo bomb behind me. News vans from all of the major Baltimore TV and radio stations were already on the scene. I considered going back, hoping there was the smallest chance that Suzanne Malveaux would be covering the story for CNN, but the rapidly growing mushroom cloud convinced me to leave.

After briefly listening to the very first radio broadcasts from the site, which included reports mentioning my office building, I called my wife, Karen, to let her know what had happened.

"I just heard about it on the news," she said. "Are you okay?"

"Yes," I said. "I'm heading home now. I'll see you soon."

That evening, when my pulse finally began to settle down, I realized how lucky I was. Fortunately, despite considerable damage to the south end of my office building, no one was hurt. Physically, the only thing that had happened to me was that the explosion had caused my penis to move from my left pant leg to my right pant leg. I knew it would return to normal at some point soon. Not bad, considering.

I called Karla and asked "Do I still have to finish watching all of the videos by tomorrow?"

"Considering that the fire marshal won't let us in the building, I'd say that's a hard no."

"Good," I said.

"You paid the truck driver to run the signal so you could get out of the videos, didn't you?" she asked mockingly.

"I did not," I said. "But it's not a bad idea for next time."

Two days later, when we were finally permitted inside the building, I knocked on Karla's office door (which was resting on the floor). When I entered, I noticed a large piece of glass sitting near her desk. We made eye contact and she said "That's the piece of the window that flew by your head and nearly decapitated you."

"Do they have any good videos for reviving someone after an office decapitation?" I asked.

"No," she admitted. "But I guess they should."

Do the events of the Day of the KABOOM have lingering results? Certainly. Ever since then, I get jumpy whenever a train explodes within two hundred yards from me. And, I always keep my keys in my pocket. The right one.

To see a video of this event that someone else posted on YouTube, go here: www.youtube.com/watch?v=VvJFe_JHED0

MurMurings

61

Have you ever met someone whose last name is Smith and you asked "are you related to (insert name here) Smith?" until you finally get one right?

Do you think food that lands on your lap feels inferior? Like it wasn't good enough to be eaten?

Advice for someone having a rough time: "You need to put one foot in front of the other."

Even better advice:
"You need to put one foot in front of the other. And keep repeating that."

I am certain I would have been a great motivational speaker.

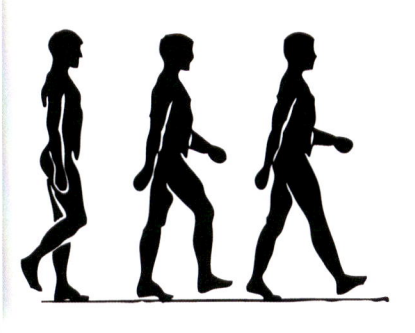

Back in the old days, why did people say hogwash? Why didn't they just say "soap"?

MurMurings

I had my garage door repaired. This is not a euphemism. And, if it was, I wouldn't even know what it would be a euphemism for.

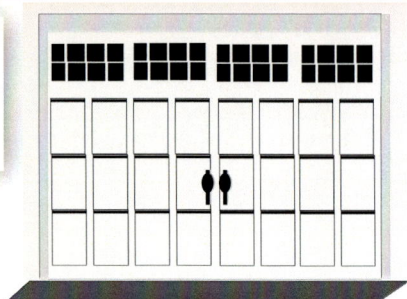

I took a quiz on the internet to figure out my elf name and then I stopped because I'm not an elf.

If you dance like no one is watching, pretty soon everyone will probably be watching. And probably pointing, too.

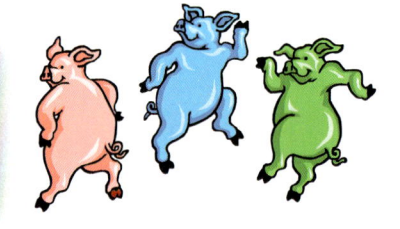

I was curious about GPS technology, so I read a few detailed articles about it on the internet.

From what I could discern, it seems to involve "science".

I got a full check up this morning. The doctor told me I'm normal. I asked for a second opinion.

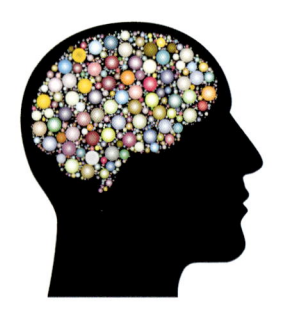

Funny Tales of Terror

9. The Time I Got Crushed By A Giant

While I don't know exactly how I threw out my back, I know it was definitely not from lifting weights, violently sneezing or fanatically licking an envelope. My working theory is that it was caused by accidentally seeing a TV ad for a chiropractor that claimed he could help people with chronic back pain. I was feeling fine before the ad; afterwards, for no apparent reason, my back went out. Way, way out. Maybe even to another time zone.

Advertising is a potent, mind-bending industry that plays on the power of suggestion and other psychological elements that induce behavioral changes. It has evolved. As a child, I would see a McDonald's ad and crave a milk shake. An advertisement-induced injury was new territory for me.

As I moaned with pain, my wife Karen came over and stood behind me to assess the situation. "Your spine is way out of alignment," she said. "You look like a crumpled up twenty-dollar bill."

Imagine that same crumpled up twenty trying to walk. That's what I looked like as I went to work that Monday morning, although I may have been a shade or two greener. But the truth was that my spine had shifted very far to the left and was causing tremendous pain.

In my office, my co-workers clearly figured out I was suffering when they saw me crying and realized that there were no movies with dead or dying sports figures, or their fathers, anywhere in the vicinity.

I'm sure you're wondering what my back has to do with a giant encounter. The answer is nothing. But, if you continue reading, you'll be rewarded soon with a real live giant. He's a literal giant, because he really exists And because he's a voracious reader. Literally.

I tried alleviating my excruciating back pain all week with stretches, medicine and rest. There was no way I would see that sumbitch chiropractor with his voodoo doll! By Friday, I felt three percent better (see Appendix for my calculation methodology), so Karen and I attended a Baltimore Orioles baseball game with a group of my industry peers. After the pregame networking happy hour ended, we went to our seats and I gingerly sat down.

"There's that crumpled five-dollar bill I lost!" a fan yelled at me. It hurt to know that I had been depreciated seventy-five percent in just a week.

Moments later one of my longtime industry friends sat down in the seat to my right. His name was Rick. Last name: "The Giant". He was 6' 11" with his shoes on. Oddly enough, he was seven feet tall with his shoes off. He once explained to me how this occurred. It was for insurance purposes.

I would have high-fived him, but in my delicate state, I couldn't jump that high. In fact, under normal conditions, I still couldn't jump that high.

"You know, Rick," I said, boldly taunting him a little. "I'm so glad you're sitting *next* to me, instead of in *front* of me."

"Fair enough," he said, "But I do enjoy a good stretch now and then."

With that, he extended his massive arms outward and leaned into me. Hard. About three hundred pounds of hard. While this might have been considered foreplay with his wife, for me it was less fun. Kind of like being T-boned by a clown car, which has to be worse than getting hit by a regular car since there are so many clowns inside. Karen could see the terror in my eyes as I wondered if Rick's weight would cause my grossly misaligned spine to simply snap. I could briefly see myself as a paraplegic, only to be interrupted by the sound of bones crunching together.

Rick, of course, had no idea of my distress. I knew he was the only thing keeping me upright, and that once he leaned away from me, I would crumble to the ground like a pile of feta cheese. And then I'd get tossed in a Greek salad. I whispered "goodbye" to Karen, knowing that I had drawn my last breath.

Rick pulled back, laughed, and said "Still glad I sat next to ya?"

It took me ten full seconds to realize I was still alive. Five more seconds went by when I determined I actually felt one hundred percent better. Rick had accidentally cured me. I felt more like a real boy than Pinocchio ever did. A faith healer, physician or witch doctor could not have done more for me than the amazing Rick The Giant.

If you ever find yourself suffering from tremendous back pain, I highly recommend Rick the Giant. Trust me, you'll be just fine.

Unless, of course, he accidentally kills you.